COACHED BY PHILIP NERI

COACHED BY PHILIP NERI

Lessons in Joy

ROB MARCO

Published by Scepter Publishers, Inc.
info@scepterpublishers.org
www.scepterpublishers.org
800-322-8773
New York

Cover Image: Detail of St. Philip Neri by Giovanni Domenico Tiepolo, oil on canvas, 1745–1749. Attributor Didier Descouens. Licensed under Creative Commons International license. https://commons.wikimedia.org.
Cover Design: Studio Red Design
Text Design and Pagination: Studio Red Design

Paperback ISBN: 978-1-59417-554-1
Ebook ISBN: 978-1-59417-555-8
Library of Congress Control Number: 2024952501

Printed in the United States of America

Contents

Foreword

One of history's greatest spectacles unfolded on a warm summer afternoon in 1973 in the tranquil town of Elmont, New York, moments before Secretariat and his rival Sham quietly entered the starting gate for a race that would crown the fastest horse in the world.

Seconds after the gates sprang open, 69,138 spectators and millions of American TV viewers saw that this Belmont Stakes had become "a match race" between two exceptional three-year-old thoroughbreds. The other colts were quickly left in their wake, swallowed by clouds of dust. By the far turn, Secretariat and Sham were all alone, straining against each other, neck-and-neck, trading the lead until the three-quarters mark. In their battle of wills, the horses had managed to set the track record for the fastest half mile opening in history. Then, something remarkable happened: Secretariat went faster.

As Jockey Ron Turcotte and his chestnut-colored colt drew away from Sham, Secretariat seemed to have transformed into Pegasus. By the top of the stretch, Sham and the rest of the field had vanished into what seemed another zip code, trailing by a few dozens of lengths. The crowd marveled, witnessing a spectacle they'd never imagined: a racehorse crossing the finish line as if in flight.

His record-time of 2:24 stands today. Horse racing enthusiasts are mostly in agreement with two events that happened that day:

1. Secretariat's startling 31-length victory in a Triple Crown race will never be broken.
2. The horse with the distinctive white blaze on his forehead established himself as the greatest racehorse in history.

After his death, an autopsy revealed that Secretariat's heart weighed 22 pounds—about 2.5 times the size of a typical thoroughbred's. Experts—trainers, jockeys, and veterinarians alike—believe this extraordinary heart allowed him to pump more blood and oxygen to his muscles during races, giving him a significant edge in speed, stamina, and power. It's a logical explanation, but I suspect something more at play. Secretariat was born with a physical anomaly, yes, but I believe his essence—his "horse sense"—instinctively knew that he was meant to *do something* with that immense heart.

It is this image of a king-sized heart I'll use to introduce you to Rob Marco's excellent work, *Coached By St. Philip Neri: Lessons in Joy*. To those unfamiliar with the extraordinary events surrounding Philip Neri, the next sentence may sound peculiar. But no one was more like Secretariat than Neri, and no one more like Neri than Secretariat. Despite their different species, they are strikingly alike—carbon copies, in their own way.

After Neri's death on May 26, 1595, at the age of seventy-nine, it was revealed that his heart, too, was more than twice the normal size. In his case, his enlarged heart was so powerful that it broke two of his ribs and caused him intense pain, unnatural heat, and severe palpitations. While immersed in prayer one day, the holy 29-year-old layman, longing for an infusion of the Holy Spirit's gifts, asked God for a pure outpouring. Thereafter, it is said, he saw a globe of fire enter his mouth, where it sank into his heart, igniting a flame that would burn for the remainder of his life.

As Secretariat became an athletic legend, joining the ranks of Babe Ruth, Muhammad Ali, and Pelé, Neri took his pure heart and became one of the Church's most celebrated saints, standing alongside his Italian contemporaries like Sts. Charles Borromeo and Aloysius Gonzaga. This is what oversized hearts are capable of and meant to do—when they are given over to their purpose.

A dark omen and sign of the times is the growing number of Catholics—perhaps even the lion's share—who might explain away Neri's "vision" and his fiery orb as mere apocrypha, his enormous heart as a biological quirk, or categorize it as a pious metaphor for a man who chose to live virtuously and, as a result, became a canonized saint. The lack of belief in the supernatural is a troubling trend these days, as more and more Catholics leave the Faith. It reflects a broader shift within the Church: a diminishing emphasis on—or even belief in—God's ability to enter into the drama of our lives through signs, healings, and miracles. It is assumed that most naysayers of Neri's miraculous heart would assent to a dead man stepping from his cave and later ascending through the sky to his Father. Jesus is God, after all. Neri, though, was just another man.

Thankfully, Rob Marco understands human beings are meant to have their ribs cracked, to be divinized by God through bursts of graces sent from heaven. St. Athanasius was clear on this, when he wrote before the Ecumenical Council in Nicaea in AD 325: "For the Son of God became man so that we might become God." The Catechism of the Catholic Church (no. 460), echoing these words, emphasized them with the writings of St. Peter: "The Word became flesh to make us 'partakers of the divine nature.'"

Outside of the finger of God, what better way to awaken a slumbering, comfortable, and technologically-addicted Western culture than through canonized saints and gifted writers like Rob Marco who choose to bring them to life?

For the past several years, I've been fortunate to call this mild-mannered, long-bearded scribe from Pennsylvania a friend. Over the last ten or fifteen years, Rob has written more words than there are in a priest's breviary—and yet, what's truly astonishing is that he never seems to run out of things to say. Each blog, book, and article strikes with a fresh and profound depth, offering something new to ponder, something to stir the soul. Marco's done it again in *Coached by Philip Neri*, as he masterfully highlights the holy aspects, mannerisms, enchanting characteristics, and charm of one of the most joy-filled saints in Church history.

In all honesty, I wanted to write this very book myself! But at the last minute, I chose a different path, deciding instead to write *Coached by the Curé,* published by Scepter this past spring. My desire was to, perhaps foolishly, give voice to St. Jean-Marie-Baptiste Vianney, the patron saint of parish priests, imagining how he might bring encouragement and hope to today's parents whose children have strayed from the faith and embraced the world. Because of his persistent cheer, though, Neri is *the* saint for the soul-depleting days of our long moral winter, and I couldn't be happier that Rob chose him to coach us to lasting joy.

The better man wrote the book on Neri, and I'll tell you why. Perhaps I reveal too much about the inner life of my friend, Rob, but for many years he has battled periodic bouts of depression and the fog of acedia through the curatives of prayer, fasting, penances, writing, and the study of scripture and the saints. This sacred medicine cabinet has allowed Rob to discover the joy and interior peace that seemed so natural to Jesus Christ and saints like St. Philip Neri. The sixteenth-century "Apostle of Joy," patron saint of cheerfulness and merriment, is the image that hangs like a portrait at the heart of Rob Marco's soul. Just as young Little Leaguers in the Bronx study the swing of Yankees slugger Aaron Judge, hoping to emulate him, Rob often turns to the icon of Neri within him for the same reason—to draw inspiration, unspoken advice, and examples of joy that transcends the struggles of life.

In a world where darkness often clouds our vision, Rob's journey toward joy—guided by Neri's example—is a reminder that it's not just about enduring the storms, but about finding a way to live as Christ wills him to. And that's precisely what Rob brings to light in his book: a lasting path to joy for readers that, despite hardships, they will see is attainable and as vibrant as ever.

I imagine I've read a few hundred books by Catholic authors, from the patristics and Augustine to the latest from Fr. Jacques Philippe and Michael O'Brien. I have never read a single writer as vulnerable as Rob Marco. He writes like a skywriter in a jet plane, humbly puffing out for the world past foibles, sinfulness, humiliations, and even his most closely guarded secrets and pains. And this is his magic. It is his gracious and masterful *trick* of fully exposing himself that sinks the hook into readers' minds and allows him to propose what a holy saint like Neri resembles. In wading into Marco's innermost thoughts and experiences, readers are exposed to what he has learned the hard way—and see clearly that he has found his footing. More accurately, God seems to have, alas, made his home in Rob's once-restless soul. He has never experienced deeper peace. It took time, though.

Marco's search for God led him to make a cross-country bike ride and into trading thoughts with a Hare Krishna group. He has slept peacefully at nights in a Benedictine monastery, where he considered becoming a monk. He battled agnosticism, discovered the unwelcome mental demons of depression and anxiety, rediscovered God, and later found himself preaching Christ, the Gospel, and Catholicism from behind a booth in the streets. He lived as a hermit on a bus and operated a Catholic Worker House, where the tinniness of prayer-thin social justice work began to pound at his conscience like endlessly howling winds.

All this said, it is because of his pursuit of God—and of attaining Neri-like joy—that has made him an expert on the fight to live as Christ for his wife and children. When he *sees* Neri leading his merry group of "Oratorians" through Rome's winding streets and filing into quiet churches to fill them with prayer and music, Rob stands among them. He takes part in their imagined storytelling, lightheartedness, and belly-laughter. He has let Philip Neri lead him by the hand into knowing the fullness of his joy, which the saint mastered. Because the author knows saints are instructors, Marco pulls up a chair, sits close, and listens.

In Philip Neri's way of thinking, his confraternity honored God not only through their study of scripture, visits to cathedrals, and attendance at Mass, but also through their leisurely lunches in sun-splashed cobblestone squares, where laughter, lively conversation, and good-natured frivolity were the order of the day. For Neri, joy was an integral part of holiness, and he saw the sacred in moments of lightheartedness and laughter.

Rob Marco understands this deeply. He knows firsthand that God often works miracles of transformation—moments of joy and light-headedness that can shift even the darkest of moods—through those who study the lives of happy saints. Their example becomes both an inspiration and a guide, showing us that holiness isn't found solely in solemnity but in the joy that radiates from a life lived fully in God's presence. For Rob, and for those who learn from Neri, joy is not just an emotion but a way to encounter the divine in every moment—whether through laughter, conversation, or simply enjoying life's small pleasures.

Marco writes: "We live in a culture in which there is a dearth of joy. We are replete in counterfeits, of course—the emptiness of superficial connections and encounters, the contraceptive nature of virtual media, the consumeristic promises proven time and time again to be empty shells and mirages. Our humor is crass and our entertainment banal, because this is what the world knows and is all it has to offer. And we accept it for lack of anything better."

The answer of course is knowing the heart of God and beginning the exacting work of coming to know him. Rob Marco understands the way to realize the fullness of his essence is by staying close to—and even writing about—delightful saints like Neri.

Because Neri asked that all of his writings be burned after his death, we mostly have just old stories of his life and the soul-saving work of his Oratory in which to remember him and pay him homage. But let us praise God for the scarcity of his recorded words, because what he has left in his wake seems more necessary at this hour where countless souls have grown numb in experiencing true inner joy. Neri's most lasting heirloom is the formation of his Oratory, which Marco called "Philip's living monument, his legacy, and the testament to his work as a disciple of Jesus Christ. The Oratory was not a school in the strict sense, nor a hospital, nor a vocation house, or charitable organization."

In *Coached by Philip Neri*, Rob reminds readers of what they, perhaps, pine for: to be part of an ever-flowing band of merry disciples living in easy joy. The West staves for an outflow of love, enlarged hearts that pour out warmth, light, charity, and the face of Christ onto lonesome streets emptied of the happy sound of children at play. Neri's "Oratorians" were the ventricles, atriums, valves, aorta, and the tens of thousands of vessels connected to the Sacred Heart, and that's why Neri's band converted countless souls. Their joy was fed by the Blood of Christ. Rome smiled again because Neri's hearty oratory forced them to. Marco writes of Neri, "This was a man who was said to have never committed a mortal sin . . . who inspired countless conversions" despite believing he was "never worthy, for I have never done any good."

That's the thing about big hearts. The larger the size, the smaller the person sees himself. Because he's always looking at himself through the light of Christ.

Rob Marco's heart is normal-sized. His racing days are over and he'll never take daily strolls down Roman streets. But he knows the deeper reason for why Secretariat couldn't be beaten. More importantly, he knows what Neri did with his enlarged heart. Rob knows that hearts are meant to be broken, in the fashion of Christ's on the Cross, who poured his out in its entirety. Ribs must crack and blood must be spilled, as Christ broke his Bread on the Cross and shed every drop of his saving Blood.

You are in safe hands with this wonderful book on Philip Neri, mostly because Rob Marco is no dummy. He knows what Christ had to say about joy and saints like Neri: "I came that they may have life, and have it abundantly" (Jn 10:10).

Kevin Wells
Author of *Coached by the Curé*
April 2025

Introduction

A young man walks the length of his college campus at midnight—lost, a little homesick, and seeking answers to questions he doesn't quite know how to ask. He wonders if studying engineering like his father is really what he wants to do, and why his favorite part of a Friday night is coming back to his dorm room after a party.

He cuts across the quad and hops the wall separating campus from the town as couples grope and stagger past him, spilling beer from red plastic Dixie cups onto the sidewalk. He sits down on a wooden bench under a row of sycamore trees when he notices an older gentleman—a professor? A "townie?"—on the other side of him reading a book under a lamppost and chuckling to himself. The young man couldn't help smiling and laughing a little himself, as the gentleman's enjoyment was almost contagious.

The gentleman must have felt the young man's eyes on him, for he looked up from his book and smiled. To the young man's surprise, he smiled back at him.

"What . . . um . . . what are you reading?" the young man asked.

"Oh, this?" the gentleman replied, still smiling and shaking his head. "Just a book of medicine."

"Oh. You are . . . a doctor, I guess?" the young man asked.

"No, no. Nothing of the sort. This is my *daily* medicine," he said, and laughed again.

"Ah, I see," the young man replied, though he didn't understand at all and was, in fact, a little puzzled.

"You look like you are missing something," the gentleman said, leveling his gaze on him with a bit more seriousness now. "What is it you are looking for out here, past midnight?"

The gentleman was disarming and warm. A bit bedraggled looking, but pleasant to talk to, the young man felt. "Oh, just . . . I don't know. I guess I just . . . just . . ." He felt tears beginning to accumulate a little in the corners of his eyes.

"We have a little gathering every Saturday afternoon on campus . . . some music, a bit of discussion, reading, and of course . . . prayer. People of all ages, and a bit of food as well. Perhaps you would like to come and see tomorrow, then?"

The young man didn't know what to say, since it was all so random, but before he could offer any resistance to the idea he simply said, "Okay."

"Very good," the gentleman said with a deep sense of affection and a playful glint in his eyes, "My name is Philip, by the way. I shall see you tomorrow then at the Oratory. I think you will find what you are looking for there."

And with this the young man watched as the older gentleman got up, opened again his book of jokes, and walked away reading it, shaking his head and laughing.

St. Philip Neri was born in Florence, Italy, in 1515. Although not much was known about his childhood, he was considered an agreeable boy ("good little Phil"). At the age of eighteen he moved to San Germano to live with his uncle and help him in his business. But the Lord God captured his heart at this age, and he left the promise of wealth and good fortune and moved to Rome shortly thereafter with not much of a plan.

Finding work and lodging as a tutor, he would frequent the public spaces in Rome seeking to interact and converse with people, a kind of "Roman Socrates" as he was known. Rome and her Christian citizens and clergy had fallen into disillusionment and, for this Philip remained in the city working for a religious revival. A contemporary of St. Ignatius of Loyola, whose acquaintance he had made, Philip lived for many years as a layman before taking holy orders in 1551 at the urging of his confessor.

It was around this time the idea of the Oratory began to take root and develop organically from his love of God and people. Praying, singing hymns, reading the scriptures and conversing about them—it was a simple and uncomplicated start to proclaiming the gospel in the Eternal City to reinvigorate its lukewarm citizens in the Faith. What once had humble and nondescript beginnings as a gathering space for faithful Catholics to grow in their faith has now spread to seventy Oratories throughout the world. The Congregation of the Oratory of St. Philip Neri is not a vowed monastic order but a "society of apostolic life"; that is, secular (meaning not belonging to a religious order, per se) priests living in community together. Oratories are independent and self-governing and based in a geographic locale.

Philip was a tireless and devoted confessor. He burned with love of God quite literally, suffering from an enlarged heart as a result of a mystical experience. He sought every opportunity for solitude and prayer, though his love of people—from the highest Vatican dignitary to the lowliest pauper—and concern for their spiritual well-being kept him both entertaining visitors and hearing their confessions. His love of God was so hard to hide that he often deflected attention from himself by making jokes, earning him a reputation for unpredictability and lightheartedness. One thing he was quite serious about, however, was the virtue of humility.

Philip died in 1595 and was canonized not long after in 1622 by Pope Gregory XV. He is the patron saint of Rome, humor, and joy.

PIPPO
BUONO
ETA
NI XV

Chapter 1

Inspiration

The Attraction to Joy

You know joy when you see it. Joy is the cousin of Christian love, for they are related and draw their lineage from the same parent. It is not fickle or prone to drought, because it draws from a deep well. If it were, it would be like a lamp that draws a flock of moths who promptly dissipate as soon as the light shuts off.

You can see the deep and steady aquifer of love in the Lord Christ when he calls his fishermen off the boat and onto land—a call antithetical to their earthly vocation. For fish live in the sea, and a man must cast off from shore, away from people, to go out and bring them in. What would draw a man without hesitation, then, to follow such an itinerant preacher with the sparse invitation, "Follow me. And I will make you fishers of men" (Mt 4:19)? We can only conclude that there is something irresistible, not only about the invitation, but the man himself.

How do James and John explain to their father—whom they have left in the lurch on the boat—that they will not be returning tomorrow or the next day, but have abandoned their vocation for good, and in an instant? They were not forced or cajoled, but drawn—by what exactly? A deceitful charm? A Ponzi-scheme promise for a better life?

Joy is a nebulous "something." It is not a bullet point list or an affection, but a field of mist that envelops a person who is unable to pocket it and take it home to show their parents. Like its older cousin Love, we are reduced to bumbling words in attempting to articulate its intoxication: "There's just . . . *something* about him," she tells her friends. As fallen creatures, we know we are susceptible to counterfeits, which leave us kneeling in the wake of hurt and shame when the light switches off.

Christian joy, however, is not of mankind, but of the Holy Spirit. Those who embody the essence of this spirit draw people to themselves because their pores exude the Spirit within them; those who do not are merely charlatans. I imagine the purity of St. Stephen, for example, filled with the Holy Spirit, who made those hardened against God cover their ears and pick up stones while onlookers witnessed the ray of light within him return to its source (see Acts 7:54–60).

While John brandished an axe in the desert drawing both the sincere and spectators alike, our Lord would not break a bruised reed or extinguish a smoldering wick as he walked (see Is 42:3). And yet John recognized him at once when Jesus came to him, not as his cousin, but as the Messiah whose way he was preparing (see Mt 3:13). Did John—of whom our Lord said there was no man greater born to mankind (see Mt 11:11)—possess this Christian joy? Of course, we know he did, and even before he was born, for as a babe he leapt "with joy" in his mother's womb from just being proximate to the still unborn Christ (see Lk 1:41). And yet would we describe John as "joyful"? Stern, perhaps. Intimidating, yes. But joyful?

Joy must go out from itself by drawing in. Every now and then and as the Lord permits, he brings into existence men and women who embody joy not only beneath the surface, but as the essence of their being and their defining trait. When we think of these men and women, we cannot distinguish that joy as separate from who they are. Joy, nourished by the wellspring of Christian love, is their embodiment, their *modus operandi*, the indelible sign that the spirit of the Lord is upon them.

Philip Neri was one of these men. Love and joy were as much an inextricable part of his being as hydrogen and oxygen are to water. And it was this joy that was the prescriptive balm of which sixteenth-century Rome was in dire need.

Born in 1515 and a Florentine through and through, Philip (baptized Filippo Romolo) was "by all accounts a handsome boy with attractive manners and a gay spirit, but sensitive—the kind that quickly wins affection from others."[1] *Gratia non tollit naturam, sed perficit,* as St. Thomas observes: "Grace does not destroy nature, but perfects it."[2] This is important to note since Philip's temperament as a boy would not experience a radical *metanoia* later in life, but rather would undergo a building of God's grace upon his human nature and for God's purposes.

There is a *naturalness* about Philip's demeanor (from the limited information we have about his character before the age of eighteen) in that he never spoke of a draw to the consecrated life and eschewed the usual customs of religious youth such as "playing the priest."[3] He was very much at home in the world of his day, while in imitation of our Lord he often "withdrew . . . to a lonely place

1. V. J. Matthews, *St. Philip Neri: Apostle of Rome and Founder of the Congregation of the Oratory* (TAN Books, 1984), pp. 22–23.

2. Thomas Aquinas, *Summa Theologica*, 1.1.8-ad2, trans. Fathers of the English Dominican Province (Benziger Bros, 1947).

3. Matthews, *St. Philip Neri,* p. 23.

apart" (Mt 14:13), consistently visiting various churches and cloisters to pray earnestly and quietly.

However, if joy is to slake its thirst and bubble over in order to wet the parched throats of the townspeople as well, you must draw from the perpetual wellspring of Love in secret, as our Lord said: "When you pray, go into your room and shut the door" (Mt 6:6). Joy's foundation was laid with the native stones of agreeableness and gaiety in Philip, but these natural attributes are not enduring enough to make a saint. For a monument to stand and to be paid homage for almost five hundred years now, as with Philip, it must be mortared and sealed with the raw material of supernatural grace.

What does it take to become joyful? Can it be taught, or "coached" as it were? If I'm being honest, I don't think it can—at least not in the way you may coach another in spiritual exercises or encourage virtues like magnanimity. For our Lord would not have counseled John, "You really should try to be more joyful in your ministry." John *was* effective, but by being who he was and sharpening his axe of repentance on a gritty whetstone.

Remember—grace builds on nature; it does not replace it. If you are not a naturally joyful person, that may be a characteristic of your temperament, not a defect of character. But that does not mean we cannot cultivate the latent seeds of joy in our hearts to the degree God ordains, seeds which are coaxed into unfurling by sunlight, moisture, and rich soil—none of which we can replicate by human means alone. It is the soil, not the seed, that we are called to build up. The only way to do that is through prayer. In this way, St. Philip can be imitated, for we can all withdraw to places set apart from time to time in order to dig our own wells.

For joy to spread as a contagion, there must be a catalyst; or, in other words, an *inspiration*. For sixteenth-century Rome, the spark of Philip's joy ignited a brush fire that may not have started were it not for the man God ordained to fan the flames of devotion in the hearts of all those in his city. Like Simon and Andrew, James and John, who dropped their nets and followed Christ because of that *something* he possessed, Philip's fellow countrymen could not resist contracting joy when they met him.

There is something in you, too, which is meant to inspire, in the way your particular time, or your particular city or town needs. The way to discover that attribute is through prayer, the door to which is barred to none by the redeeming grace of Christ—Philip's own inspiration—loving, forgiving, and dying for *all* mankind. Including you.

Whether or not you are a naturally joyful person is beside the point—there is something about you that reflects God's glory, a glory which cannot be painted with a single brush or pigment. Sin is a repellent not only to grace, but to those who seek to bask in the light of grace. But for those who hoe a row for virtue in the garden of their hearts, consistently weeding and tilling the soil, they will draw all people to themselves as Christ did and reap a bountiful harvest (see Jn 12:32).

In Practice, Joyful Contagion

1. Whether or not we are a naturally joyful person, we are all called to "cultivate the latent seeds of joy in our hearts." The "coaching" towards a joyful disposition comes through our own cultivation. What are ways that you cultivate the seeds of joy in your heart in your daily life?
2. "Philip's joy ignited a brush fire." The spark of our joy must originate from our love for the Lord. Examine your heart. Do you foster a joy that has its roots in your love of God?
3. "There is something in you, too, which is meant to inspire." When examining your heart, can you pinpoint your God-given attributes that can be better used to inspire others? What virtues must you cultivate to make these qualities bring glory to God?

Chapter 2

All Things to All Men

Nothing Was Too High for Him, Nothing Too Low

Paul the Apostle was a master evangelist. He brought the same gusto to spreading "the Way" that he did to his efforts to snuff it out. Whether it was apostolic zeal, single-minded obsessiveness, or the cognizant weight of his debt to the crucified Christ who opened his eyes on the road to Damascus, we would be hard-pressed to find a more zealous promoter of Christian doctrine and practice throughout history. He simply could not rest until not just Rome, but the whole world, was converted to Christ.

When Paul wrote to the Christian churches that were being established, it is important to note that he didn't write one epistle, copy it, and send it to each individual community like some kind of generalized proclamation. He tailored each individual letter, addressed to the hearts and minds of these very different communities of believers, each with their own cultures, backgrounds, and particular issues. Though he was stalwart in preaching about Christ and Christ crucified to all mankind, the apostle recognized that some believers were still suckling at the teat while others needed meat (see 1 Cor 3:2). When it came to eating food offered to idols (though he makes clear that an idol has no real existence), to those of weak conscience, he vowed, for their sake, never to eat meat, lest he cause his brother to fall (see 1 Cor 8:4–13). Though unwavering in his upholding of true doctrine, in the particulars that were ancillary to the faith he afforded liberty for the sake of unity.

When I was in college, there was a pastor of a local church known as "The Willard Preacher" (so nicknamed because he had been preaching outside the Willard building on campus every day, rain or shine, since 1982). He was a "fire and brimstone" type, engaging students with the same message day in and day out of the need for repentance. To my knowledge, his preaching was always consistent, with very little deviation. For many students, though, his outpost became a kind of "white noise," the way you would get daily spam messages that you just automatically deleted or left unread. I don't know how many converts to the Christian faith he made, but one thing was for sure: he was single-minded in his desire to lead people to Christ.

You could say Philip, too, possessed this single-mindedness when it came to the salvation of souls. But his methodology was markedly different. He embodied a pliability in his demeanor, of meeting people where they were and gently leading them to come to faith. Though he initially (and fervently) desired to be a missionary to the Indies, he was told by a holy Cistercian that "Rome is to be your Indies."[4] And so in Rome he stayed, lodging in a small room near the piazza of St. Eustachio for most of his early life.[5]

But Philip would not mark out an outpost in the city like an urban St. Simeon Stylites[6] and have people come to him; quite the opposite in fact. It was known that Philip had an ardent love of charity and so would frequently visit the sick in hospitals—sweeping floors, feeding and washing patients, and making sure they received the sacraments. He would also visit with beggars and idlers on the streets, as well as warehouse workers and others employed in the city, and seek to lead them to greater virtue. It is important to note that at this time in

4. Matthews, *St. Philip Neri,* p. 15.
5. Matthews, *St. Philip Neri,* p. 32.
6. St. Simeon Stylites the Elder was a Syrian ascetic who lived on a platform on top of a pillar for thirty-six years.

his life, Philip was still a layman and had not taken holy orders. And yet his conversions were effective in this state because he had gained a reputation for being a virtuous and genuinely spiritual man.

> Nothing was too high for him, nothing too low. He taught poor begging women to use mental prayer; he took out boys to play; he protected orphans; he acted as novice-master to the children of St. Dominic. He was the teacher and director of artisans, mechanics, cashiers in banks, merchants, workers in gold, artists, men of science. He was consulted by monks, canons, lawyers, physicians, courtiers; ladies of the highest rank, convicts going to execution, engaged in their turn his solicitude and prayers. Cardinals hung about his room, and Popes asked for his miraculous aid in disease, and his ministrations in death. It was his mission to save men, not from, but in, the world.[7]

Philip had a "by whatever means necessary" approach to winning souls "as the magnet draws iron,"[8] but he always tailored it to a particular person's dispositions. He could be subtle and gentle or physical and shocking, depending on the circumstance.

7. John Henry Newman, "Sermon 12, The Mission of Philip—Part 2," no. 239, in *The Newman Reader*, National Institute for Newman Studies, https://newmanreader.org/works/occasions/sermon12-2.html.

8. Newman, "Sermon 12:2," no. 237.

There is a story of an ambitious young man, Francesco Zazzara, who came to Philip with his aspirations to study law, telling him of all his grand plans, which Philip listened to and affirmed in earnest, until he landed the fatal blow to the excited young man's conscience in the form of a question: "And then?" The question lodged in his mind for days like a splinter that could not be extracted. *And then?* And it was not just the question itself that Philip posed, but the way in which he posed it—tenderly and without judgment. The man eventually abandoned his career and joined Philip's congregation, where he remained until his death.[9]

In another instance, which called for a less-than-gentle approach, he took an unrepentant criminal by the collar and put him on his back forcefully. It shocked the criminal enough to be moved to confess his sins and receive absolution before facing his death sentence.[10]

There are many other examples, from those suffering scruples to the spiritually lukewarm, in which God graced Philip with a keen intuition into human nature—not just of humanity in general, but of human persons in their particularity. Philip poured himself out as an offering to those he ministered to, even to the detriment of his own health later in life, as St. Paul did: "To the

9. Matthews, *St. Philip Neri,* p. 133.
10. Matthews, *St. Philip Neri,* pp. 140–141.

weak I became weak, that I might win the weak. I have become all things to all men, that I might by all means save some" (1 Cor 9:22).

In this, Philip maintained the utmost respect for human freedom and diversity of character. "There are Saints," says Cardinal Newman, "whose mission lies rather in separating off from each other the world and the Truth; that of other Saints lies in bringing them together. Philip's was the latter."[11]

In the same vein as St. Augustine's famous maxim, "Love and do what you will,"[12] even to those who disrupted his coveted quiet time alone in his room, Philip replied, "They may chop wood on my back, so long as they do not sin."[13]

Likewise, in contrast to the various schools of mystical theology that were beginning to rise up in his day, Philip was reluctant to lay out a particular methodology or "way" of praying. "Be humble and obedient and the Holy Ghost will teach you," he would say when people asked him how to make mental prayer.[14] Mortification and prayer, for

11. Newman, "Sermon 12:2," no. 222.

12. "*Dilige et quod vis fac,*" also presented as "*Ama et fac quod vis,*" in Augustine of Hippo, *In Epistolam Joannis ad Parthos*, tract. 7, sec. 8, in *Nicene and Post-Nicene Fathers*, First Series, vol. 7, ed. Philip Schaff, trans. H. Browne and Joseph H. Myers (Buffalo, NY: Christian Literature Publishing Co., 1888), 466, https://www.ccel.org/ccel/schaff/npnf107.

13. Matthews, *St. Philip Neri,* p. 113.

14. Matthews, *St. Philip Neri,* p. 153.

Philip, went hand in hand. But just how people mortified themselves most effectively would be different for each individual under Philip's gentle hand.

What, then, does it mean to "become all things to all men"? In the first place, we cannot take ourselves too seriously or hold ourselves in too high a regard. Like Christ, who "emptied himself, taking the form of a servant" (Phil 2:7), Philip did not hold himself too attached to his own will and ways. If he was wanted, drawing himself away from his room of prayer, he would oblige, "leaving Christ for Christ," as he would say.[15] And he was keenly aware that he had never done any good in his own eyes, and everyone was better than him. "If you were one day to see me whipped through the streets you would say, 'Ah! Look at that fellow Philip who pretended to be so spiritual, give it him well.'"[16]

It's worth stating again: Don't take yourself too seriously. In Philip's view, a person who cannot endure a loss of honor is not capable of progressing in the spiritual life. As we will see in the next chapter, Philip liberally employed humor and self-deprecation as spiritual instruments not only to win souls, but to keep his own feet planted here on earth.

15. Matthews, *St. Philip Neri,* p. 151.
16. Matthews, *St. Philip Neri,* p. 156.

In Practice, Joyful Availability

1. "Philip did not hold himself too attached to his own will and ways." This difficult task, to place God's will above our own, can at times feel daunting. Do you present this level of detachment when God is clearly calling you to place his will before your own?
2. Cardinal Newman alleged that St. Philip brought the world and the truth together. This implies an attitude of seeing God's beauty and truth all around him. Are you able to see God shining through, even in the bleakest moments? Do you have a mirthful disposition that allows you to see God working all around you, even amidst chaos or sin?
3. "Philip poured himself out as an offering." Do you present this level of availability to those around you? What are ways in which you can be more available to your family and loved ones as a loving offering?

PHILIPPUS NERIUS
Theol. Pontificius.

Chapter 3

Crucifying Pretensions

The Unconventional Path

The Church recognizes that there exist "those elements of truth and grace which are found among peoples, and which are, as it were, a secret presence of God."[17] The West does not have an exclusive hold on claiming wise men and holy ascetics throughout history. Take for instance the *yuródivyy* ("holy fool") in the Orthodox tradition, who voluntarily adopts the guise of insanity or uncouth disagreeableness to conceal their sanctity and avoid adulation. Or the Zen masters of the non-Christian East, who seek to short-circuit the rational mind of their students and lead them to enlightenment through riddles known as *koans*—and sometimes even with a good beating!

17. *Catechism of the Catholic Church* (United States Conference of Catholic Bishops, 1997), no. 856.

In one such story the Zen master Hakuin was known for living a pure life. When a beautiful girl in the village was found to be with child, her parents pressed her on who the father was, and she named Hakuin. When they approached him in anger, he simply responded, "Is that so?" The child was brought to Hakuin, who had lost his reputation by this time, but he took good care of the child, obtaining milk and everything else the child needed. A year later the girl, racked by her conscience, told her parents the truth—that the real father was a young man who worked in the fish market. They rushed to Hakuin, apologizing and asking his forgiveness while imploring him for the child back. In yielding the child to them, all he said was, "Is that so?"[18]

Holy fools in the Christian West are not as well-known or common—we may think of St. Francis of Assisi stripping naked in front of his bishop before renouncing the world, for one. But this may be due in part to the heavy influence of Scholasticism, which supports a more rational and measured approach to saintly living.

Philip Neri was a man, however, who defied convention. He was an Italian and a Roman Catholic, with feet firmly planted in the sixteenth-century West. So buoyant was his love of God and his desire to bring all

18. Paul Reps, *Zen Flesh, Zen Bones: A Collection of Zen and Pre-Zen Writings* (Anchor Books, 1961), pp. 7–8.

people to God that, as was noted in previous chapters, he employed a "by whatever means necessary" approach to caring for his disciples in the school of sanctity that was sometimes unconventional.

And yet his methodology, which seems to defy sensibility, has a rich tradition in the Church Fathers. St. John Climacus in the seventh century considered vainglory the mother of pride and its forerunner, for "vainglory induces pride in the favored and resentment in those who are slighted." In *The Ladder of Divine Ascent*, he wrote:

> When you hear that your neighbour or friend has abused you behind your back or even to your face, then show love and praise him. It is a great work to shake from the soul the praise of men, but to reject the praise of demons is greater. It is not he who depreciates himself who shows humility (for who will not put up with himself?) but he who maintains the same love for the very man who reproaches him.[19]

In the same vein, St. John Cassian, in the fifth century, considered the demon of self-esteem to be "a multi-form and subtle passion which is not readily perceived even by the person whom it tempts." He goes on,

19. John Climacus, *The Ladder of Divine Ascent,* trans. Archimandrite Lazarus Moore (Harper & Brothers, 1959), pp. 73–74.

> When it cannot seduce a man with extravagant clothes, it tries to tempt him by means of shabby ones. When it cannot flatter him with honour, it inflates him by causing him to endure what seems to be dishonour. When it cannot persuade him to feel proud of his display of eloquence, it entices him through silence into thinking he has achieved stillness. When it cannot puff him up with the thought of his luxurious table, it lures him into fasting for the sake of praise.[20]

Philip the teacher was keenly aware of who the enemy was and knew with deadly seriousness the potential for pride and vainglory to pull down his disciples (and himself) from the upper rungs of the ladder leading heavenward. Despite the seriousness of these pernicious demons and vices, however, Philip employed a most *unserious* way of inoculating against its poison. One disciple was made to wear a fur cloak through the summer; another was made to dance in the refectory in the presence of distinguished guests.

One particularly gifted preacher—Fr. Agostino Manni, who belonged to Philip's Congregation—was esteemed for his beautiful sermons. To thwart the demon of vainglory from taking root in him and to mortify his pretenses, Philip ordered the priest to deliver the same

20. John Cassian, "On The Eight Vices," in *The Philokalia: The Complete Text*, ed. G. E. H. Palmer et al., vol. 1 (Faber and Faber, 1979), p. 91.

discourse six times in a row without changing a word, so that eventually those who heard him would now murmur, "Here comes the Father who has only got one sermon."[21]

According to Philip, there are four steps in humility: "To despise the world, to despise no man, to despise oneself and to despise being despised."[22] This last step is a curious one, a kind of non sequitur that may give some insight into a saint that eschewed a kind of logical piety in favor of the seemingly nonsensical. For we know our Lord was "despised and rejected by men . . . he was despised, and we esteemed him not" (Is 53:3). Why would Philip advise those who wished to be schooled in humility to "despise being despised" when it seemed congruent with our Lord being despised?

One Zen saying goes, "If you meet the Buddha on the road, kill him!" Philip's famous maxim, "Let no one wear a mask, otherwise he will do ill; and if he has one, let him burn it"[23] seems in the same vein—getting to the heart of things beneath the surface. For God is not a God of pretensions.

In Philip there is perhaps a little bit of the nonsensical character of the exacting Master of the Orient, who deftly brings his disciple to enlightenment with a kind

21. Matthews, *St. Philip Neri,* pp. 165–167.

22. Matthews, *St. Philip Neri,* p. 158.

23. Philip Neri, *The Maxims and Sayings of St. Philip Neri,* trans. F. W. Faber (St. Athanasius Press, 2009); excerpts found at www.liturgialatina.org/oratorian/maxims.htm.

of riddle that, like a flash of lightning, severs the pupil's *idea* of holiness in favor of the real thing and leaves him forever changed. An example of this is when a priest was kicked out of the Congregation by Philip and was never told his perceived fault. For days Philip never budged, but then suddenly said he forgave him and that "he must never behave like that again." Just what it was he did would forever remain a mystery to the grateful yet bewildered priest.[24]

The Holy Spirit was not called a "wild goose" by the early Christians for no reason. For as John the Evangelist, who wrote in a different vein from the Synoptic authors, recognized, "The wind blows where it wills, and you hear the sound of it, but you do not know whence it comes or whither it goes; so it is with every one who is born of the Spirit" (Jn 3:8).

It can be a temptation for the Catholic striving toward holiness on his own today to think in terms of linear equations of holiness. "If I just do X in a spirit of Y, I will attain Z." We often do not see our own blind spots—whether it be vainglory, pride, or other pernicious vices living beneath the surface. You may even recognize this and be looking for spiritual direction, for which there are so few trained guides.

24. Matthews, *St. Philip Neri,* p. 167.

Philip, for his part, was a master of human and spiritual intuition. He knew the principal enemies of progress in the spiritual life, and he was not averse to using a variety of methods to root out whatever kept someone from growing in holiness. He also knew holiness was not an equation or formula, and so his spiritual prescriptions varied from person to person in order to put to death whatever was standing between them and sainthood.

We can see an example of the deftness of a skilled teacher and the malleability of a bull-headed teenager trying to DIY his way to heaven in the story of Sts. Robert Bellarmine and Aloysius Gonzaga. Aloysius was a contemporary of Philip, as well as an Italian, and later recognized as a saint. When Aloysius entered the Jesuits at the age of seventeen, he was appointed a spiritual director, St. Robert Bellarmine. Levelheaded and patient, Bellarmine listened to Aloysius describe his extreme schedule of individual religious practice . . . then ordered him to cease it. He was assigned instead to work at a local hospital tending to the sick and infirm. Squeamish, he was repulsed by the work, and he disliked people, which is probably why he was initially inclined to his private devotions and mortifications. When the plague hit Rome in January 1591, the sick and dying were everywhere, overwhelming the hospitals, and Alyosius had to dig deep and draw on that Italian stubbornness and bulldog-like willpower to stomach the work.

But in time, by God's grace, a transformation happened. Though this was never work he would have chosen for himself, Aloysius began to see Christ in the sick and dying, similar to St. Francis's encounter with the leper. He experienced compassion for them, and often carried them from the streets to the hospital on his back. He contracted the plague as a result, and died at the age of twenty-three.

Training in the school of the saints can be more art than exact science. Philip shows us that we need teachers, yes, but not necessarily those with PhDs in mystical theology. A holy person with the gift of intuition is worth all the weight of many textbooks, because they are a doctor that knows the landscape of the soul. And as we will see in the next chapter, laughter is sometimes the best medicine.

In Practice, Joyful Unpretentiousness

1. "Vainglory induces pride in the favored and resentment in those who are slighted." As enemies of humility and unpretentiousness, vanity and pride have an all-too-tight hold on the world. What are ways in which you can imagine your embrace of unpretentiousness working to counteract this grip?

2. Unpretentiousness includes seeing God at work in every heart. "The missionary task implies a *respectful dialogue* with those who do not yet accept the Gospel. Believers can profit from this dialogue by learning to appreciate better 'those elements of truth and grace which are found among peoples, and which are, as it were, a secret presence of God'" (*Catechism*, no. 856). Do you believe in the "secret presence of God" in the hearts of others? Does this belief instill in you a compassion and respect in your dealings with others who do not believe in the gospel? If not, how can you foster more respect?

3. "Philip shows us that we need teachers, yes, but not necessarily those with PhDs in mystical theology." Do you believe unpretentiously that, rooted in the Holy Spirit, you can be a conduit of transformation in others' lives?

Chapter 4

Holy Wit

If You Don't Laugh, You'll Cry

I have a confession: I love to laugh. Whether it's skillful stand-up comedy, a well-written sitcom, or even slapstick humor, I simply can't imagine going through life without having something to make me laugh from time to time. When my now-wife and I were dating, a sense of humor was one of the top three qualities I was looking for in a partner. I think people underestimate how important humor and the ability to laugh at ourselves can be in lubricating the engine of marriage and getting through the hard stuff.

In the hierarchy of human needs, laughter does not seem to rank near the top alongside basics such as food, shelter, clothing, safety, and security. Like music and the arts (which are usually the first programs to be cut from school budgets), humor is oftentimes considered a "non-essential," even by many Christians. While this is true on a surface level in terms of sheer survival, I wouldn't want to live in a world without laughter any more than I would want to subsist on leafy greens for the rest of my life. I don't think you would either.

We simply cannot write about St. Philip Neri without introducing to the reader the holy virtue of humor. But for Philip, humor was not laughter for its own sake but always for divine and human purposes alike, a strand in his net for catching souls. As we will also see in this chapter, laughter and humor were also necessary medicines for keeping Philip himself grounded here on earth.

For laughter and wit to be employed in the school of virtue, you must first possess such virtue as a prerequisite, lest you be considered simply a buffoon or jokester. Philip had the necessary "street cred" as a holy and genuinely spiritual man, so that his joking and laughter were used to grease the skids of grace and bring others to conversion.

Lest you think Philip was a kind of sixteenth-century "merry prankster," I can assure you he was nothing of the sort. It is important not to confuse laughter for its own sake with *lightheartedness*—a quality which Philip most certainly possessed. Philip's friend, Fabrizio de' Massimi, noted, "He was so affectionate that he drew all the world after him in the most wonderful way imaginable."[25]

25. Matthews, *St. Philip Neri,* p. 149.

Lightheartedness has a way of putting people at ease. His desire was for all mankind to know the love of God which so fervently burned within him, and this gentle affability drew others to himself so that he might share some of that warmth.

But where others received the heat from the hearth of Philip's spirit, it was not as easy for him to temper its flames which threatened to consume his own heart. For the sake of his health, or even to enable sleep, it was sometimes necessary to distract himself with a book of jokes to keep him from being swept up in ecstasy. This burning love in his chest was far from figurative, as we will see in a later chapter, for his heart had physically swollen by the grace of the Holy Spirit.

In this we can note an interesting observation, which applies to all—single and married, religious and lay—and that is that laughter can be a vital "bleed valve" to release the pressure cooker that life can sometimes put us in. As a priest friend of mine used to say, "If you don't laugh, you'll cry." We are not meant to go full-throttle and redline through life without both leisure and laughter from time to time. It is a kind of God-given reset that keeps marriages healthy, vocations fruitful, and work from becoming drudgery.

There is nothing shameful about humor and laughter in the life of a Christian, provided it does not detract from the glory of God. We can do this because we know, by the grace of our baptism, that the devil holds no power over us, for Christ has won the victory. G. K. Chesterton wrote, "It is the test of a good religion whether you can joke about it."[26]

It is not even unwise to laugh (even out loud!) in the face of the devil's tiresome temptations when we are safe within the mantles of Christ and Our Lady, because the devil himself knows he is on a short leash. As the great St. Thomas More said, "The devil, the proud spirit, cannot endure to be mocked."[27] Those who do not have such confidence cannot laugh, "but the Lord laughs at the wicked, for he sees that his day is coming" (Ps 37:13).

We, however, can share in this laughter and confidence as adopted sons and daughters because we are heirs slated for a divine inheritance. "If God be with us, there is no one else left to fear," according to Philip.[28] Additionally, the ability to laugh and make light of things is an indication of a deeper joy that is confident and sure of itself. Those who have trouble doing so can even doubt the goodness of a Creator who has even the very hairs on our heads counted (see Mt 10:30). We need not be fearful

26. *G. K. Chesterton,* "Spiritualism," in *All Things Considered* (Methuen & Co., 1908), https://www.gutenberg.org/ebooks/11505.

27. Thomas More, *A Dialogue of Comfort Against Tribulation* (London: Richard Tottel, 1553), bk. 2, sec. 16.

28. Neri, *The Maxims.*

or anxious. We can laugh because the Father desires for us to cast our cares on him, for he cares for us (see 1 Pt 5:7).

Did the Lord Jesus ever laugh? While we do not see any explicit indication of this in Scripture, that should not rule out the possibility. Laughter, like weeping, is a normal human emotion, and we are human beings just as Christ had a human nature. We should avoid such Jansenist or Puritanical tendencies to consider laughter and wit as incompatible with Catholicism. "Serve the Lord with laughter," Padre Pio (a most serious saint) has been quoted as saying. Joy is like the protein that sustains us for the long haul, while laughter is akin to the carbohydrates our bodies need for energy in the short term.

Philip's joy was an indication of his deep confidence in God, and his laughter like an alarm meant to drive away those who would seek to steal it. We, too, should not be afraid to laugh, for a lighthearted person tends to attract people. In drawing people to himself as Christ did, Philip is simply reflecting that good nature which comes from God himself.

Take a lesson from Philip's life of holy wit and give yourself permission to laugh. It is sanctioned by God, supported by the Faith, and approved by the Church. Embrace it, and don't fear. A hearty guffaw or a lighthearted chuckle can do more for your health than pills and prescriptions. It's free, and it's good for the soul.

It puts people at ease and oftentimes a smile on their face. If joy is the sun which illuminates everything, laughter is the warmth from its rays which coaxes a person to take off their coat, relax, and stay a while.

In Practice, Joyful Wit

1. Do you believe in "the holy virtue of humor"? That you can bring others to the truth of the gospel through joyful wit? What are ways in which you can infuse the virtue of humor into your day-to-day living and your interactions, to the benefit of others?
2. "The ability to laugh and make light of things is an indication of a deeper joy that is confident and sure of itself." Conversely, a joyful laugh can help bring levity to a tired or weary soul. Examine the chambers of sadness that dwell in your heart, and practice bringing joy to those dark corners by welcoming thoughts of gladness, comfort, and gratitude.
3. Laughter "is sanctioned by God, supported by the Faith, and approved by the Church." How can you make room in your life for more laughter? What attitudes do you have to let go of in order to be more receptive to the holy virtue of humor?

Chapter 5

Withdrawing to a Lonely Place

Until I Was Alone, I Never Really Lived

"He who does not pray will certainly be damned."[29]

St. Alphonsus does not mince words here, but the *Catechism* is no less exacting:

> *Prayer is a vital necessity*. Proof from the contrary is no less convincing: if we do not allow the Spirit to lead us, we fall back into the slavery of sin. How can the Holy Spirit be our life if our heart is far from him?[30]

Prayer is indeed a vital necessity in the life of a Christian. You can be a Christian without laughing, or even engaging with the world (as the eremitic life

29. "*Del gran mezzo della preghiera*." Alphonsus Liguori in *Catechism,* no. 2744.
30. *Catechism,* no. 2744.

attests). But you simply cannot be considered a Christian of any worth if you do not pray regularly. Prayer is the oxygen in our blood without which the organs simply cease functioning.

Because all the saints sought to imitate Christ and walk in his footsteps, we are on solid ground when we study the Scriptures and do the same. And we can see the nature of Jesus Christ in that he walked among men, but often communed with his Father in heaven apart from them:

> And after he had dismissed the crowds, he went up into the hills by himself to pray. When evening came, he was there alone. (Mt 14:23)
>
> In these days he went out into the hills to pray; and all night he continued in prayer to God. (Lk 6:12)
>
> But so much the more the report went abroad concerning him; and great multitudes gathered to hear and to be healed of their infirmities. But he withdrew to the wilderness and prayed. (Lk 5:15–16)

Philip's life was marked by this imitation of our Lord in withdrawing to quiet places apart from others to pray and be alone with God, even as a young man. Whether it was the chapel at Monte Cassino in the fissure of a mountain, or the catacombs of San Sebastiano, he loved to pray and seek solitude in these reclusive places.

In fact, he spent the majority of his early life as a layman before his ordination as a quasi-hermit—praying for hours on end, while retaining his room at San Girolamo. It was not hard for him to pray, either. It came naturally to him, as naturally as his character. Philip loved to pray because he was consumed by love, and the trifles of the world paled in comparison to the joy of communion with God.

The Christian call to charity is somewhat of a catch-22: we are called to be *in* the world, but not of it. We are called to love others without seeking to also possess them. Christ walked among the people and gave himself as a friend to his apostles, but also lamented that he had no lasting place to lay his head (see Mt. 8:20). In Christ we see a heart that rests with the people of his day; he weeps over them, caring as a mother hen (see Lk 13:34 and 19:41). But while his heart is with the people, his soul is knit to the Father. Christ goes out from solitude—to eat, to heal, to preach, and teach—but returns to it time and time again to be fortified and renewed in prayer. "Therefore, our Lord and His angels will draw near and abide with those who, for the love of virtue, withdraw themselves from their acquaintances and from their worldly friends," says Thomas à Kempis. "It is better that a man be solitary and take good heed of himself than that, forgetting himself, he perform miracles in the world."[31]

There is also something of a betrayal of ourselves when we associate too closely with the world; it is as if we forget ourselves, becoming like the man who looks at himself in the mirror but then goes away and forgets what he looks like (see Jas 1:23–24). When we are alone, we cannot hide. We are naked in consciousness before the Lord, who sees all things (see Prv 15:3). Wise people see themselves for who they are, but this is not possible when they are constantly surrounded by the company of others and never alone. Bl. Paolo Giustiniani notes, "Until I was alone, I never really lived. Until I was alone, I was not with myself. Until I was alone, I never drew near to my creator."[32]

The world today is uncomfortable with aloneness. Perhaps that is even an understatement. The world today is *afraid* to be alone. Because when we are alone, we are with ourselves—and we don't always like who that is. When Philip went off to pray in lonely places, it was not to endure the burden of solitude, but to bask in the joy of communion with his Creator.

31. Thomas à Kempis, *The Imitation of Christ*, (Image Books, 1989), p. 57.

32. The Congregation of St. Romuald, *A Prayer of Blessed Paul Giustiniani,* accessed March 25, 2025, https://stromuald.weebly.com.

As servants of the King, we share in his joy when we are faithful in our service (see Mt 25:23). If you want to imitate Christ and learn the secret of joy, learn to be alone as Christ was so often alone. Resist the urge for constant connection with the world, and rest awhile with the Father who is everything, everywhere. "Whither shall I go from thy spirit? Or whither shall I flee from thy presence? If I ascend to heaven, thou art there! If I make my bed in Sheol, thou art there!" (Ps 139:7–8).

The Lord waits for you. Seek him while he still may be found (see Is 55:6).

In Practice, Joyful Prayer

1. "If we do not allow the Spirit to lead us, we fall back into the slavery of sin. How can the Holy Spirit be our life if our heart is far from him?" Do you set aside time for silent prayer, in which nothing is read or said, but you make yourself present to the Lord? If at times you have fallen away from the practice of silence and prayer, do you see the adverse effects in your life?
2. "When we are alone, we cannot hide. We are naked in consciousness before the Lord, who sees all things." Are you afraid or uncomfortable with silence or aloneness? Or do you find comfort in being fully seen, known, and loved by the Lord?
3. "If you want to imitate Christ and learn the secret of joy, learn to be alone as Christ was so often alone." When in silence with the Lord, do you fall into melancholy, overcome with burden, or do you present yourself joyfully to the Lord? How can you infuse more joy into your aloneness with Christ?

Chapter 6

Lay Informality

The Domestic Oratory

In our home, we regularly practice what we refer to as "scruffy hospitality." This involves inviting a friend, acquaintance, or stranger over to tea or a meal without any pre-planning or fanfare. Sometimes there is minimal food or ingredients for a meal in the cupboard, but that is regarded more as a challenge than an impediment to having company over—we simply whip up something with what we have on hand. As the saying goes, "Food is the icing, and company is the cake."

There is a great freedom here with definitive advantages—the lack of formality and temptation to "put on airs" makes a hospitable environment for informal conversation where guests can "come as they are." It also means that we don't have to stress about "getting something on the calendar" weeks in advance. The perfect is the enemy of the good, and because there is no illusion of being a grand event, we are more inclined to host in this way. Plus, my wife and I are not very formal people—we simply do what we feel called to do with what we have.

Part of this is for our own benefit of course (we enjoy people), but we also see it as part of our calling as Christians to open our home as a kind of "domestic oratory" in which to live out the works of mercy at the kitchen table: counseling the doubtful, instructing the ignorant, comforting the sorrowful. Our guest may be a new face at church, a coworker, or even a relative stranger—people we encounter in our daily lives. Because there is no expectation or formal commitment involved, there is freedom to accept or decline without pressure. But the invitation is always there.

Informality may be considered a particular character trait of Philip that lent itself to his mission of bringing souls out of tepidity and into deep waters. But because grace perfects nature, as St. Thomas says, we can see that Philip's informal way of being was not a lack or defect, but at the heart of his mission. St. Cardinal John Henry Newman said of Philip,

> He contemplated as the idea of his mission, not the propagation of the faith, nor the exposition of doctrine, nor the catechetical schools; whatever was exact and systematic pleased him not; he put

> from him monastic rule and authoritative speech, as David refused the armor of his king. . . .
>
> He came to the Eternal City and he sat himself down there, and his home and his family gradually grew up around him, by the spontaneous accession of materials from without. He did not so much seek his own as draw them to him. He sat in his small room, and they in their gay, worldly dresses, the rich and the wellborn, as well as the simple and the illiterate, crowded into it.[33]

There was in fact a particular draw to Philip's informal spirit, since it stood in stark contrast to the spirit of the age in sixteenth-century Rome. Whereas power, politics, and worldly prestige were at the forefront of life in Italian society, Philip drew people to himself through a warm affection and a "personalist" approach centuries before Pope St. John Paul II popularized the term.

To Philip, the time to start "doing good" was now, and that charge was made to clergy and laypersons alike. Though he desired to remain in the lay state, he was urged by his confessor to pursue holy orders and was ordained in 1551 at the age of thirty-six. Prior to that he had already accomplished a considerable amount as a layman.

33. John Henry Newman, *The Idea of a University* (Longmans, Green, and Co., 1902), Discourse IX, sec. 9, pp. 235–236.

Philip's ministry was a kind of active-contemplative fusion. He was concerned for the needs of the poor, of pilgrims, and the infirmed, and his charisma was such that he drew others into undertaking the work of charity at the hospital Santa Trinità, if for no other reason than Philip himself inspiring such work. But such charity was a vehicle, a way of "doing good" and exercising the work of virtue, the structure of an outward facing building built on the foundation of prayer.

We sometimes think we need to wait for permission to do good, that if this or that work is not officially sanctioned or comes from some formal organization, we cannot carry it out. That is nonsense. There is no prohibition against speaking with people about the gospel, against being merry and living out the joy instilled in us at our baptism. Whether it is at a church or someone's house, the encouragement to do good often lies fallow because no one takes up the plow to start the work.

Philip was a man who inspired, who naturally drew out the best in people, and he did so by capitalizing on that spirit of informality as a layman (and later as a priest) to start where people were, to work with what they had, to provide not just prohibitions but healthy alternatives to sin and vice.

The purpose of this "going out" to do good, in the way God ordains, is not to bolster one's spiritual resume or simply occupy time in activity, but to have a well-rounded, zealous spiritual life pleasing to God. Prayer, spiritual reading, discussion, music, charity—Philip made use of all these things for himself, of course, but he also made them attractive and nourishing for others.

No doubt his efforts were aided by divine grace, but the work itself was an exercise of the will, a willingness to take a chance and potentially look foolish. Philip was inspired by the Holy Spirit, and in turn inspired others by his living out of that calling. You, too, have a calling. Whether that is to lead or to support, there is no shortage of work in the vineyard of the Lord. He needs laborers who respond without delay. Will you be one of them?

In Practice, Joyful Informality

1. "Scruffy hospitality" creates "a hospitable environment for informal conversation where guests can 'come as they are.'" In a world of flaunting perfection, do you have a hard time letting go? Has this become an impediment to friendships and an inhibitor to evangelism in your life?
2. "Philip drew people to himself through a warm affection and a 'personalist' approach." How personable and approachable are you to others? Do you emit a warm and hospitable attitude? In what ways can you let your guard down, thus allowing Christ to use you as his conduit?
3. Philip's charitable work was a "vehicle, a way of 'doing good' and exercising the work of virtue, the structure of an outward facing building built on the foundation of prayer." What are my motivations in my acts of charity and almsgiving? Do I root all my good works in my prayer with the Lord?

Chapter 7

Apostle of the Here and Now

When Shall We Begin to Do Good?

When Philip would ask his companions, "Well, my brothers, when shall we begin to do good?" the implication of course was that the time to begin doing good was *now*. Why put off until tomorrow what you can do today? As Philip would say, "We must not be behind time in doing good; for death will not be behind his time."[34] It's a good, practical way of approaching life and yet you would be surprised how many people get into the refrain of "I'll do it tomorrow," when tomorrow is never promised to come.

In the Book of James, we see this:

> Come now, you who say, "Today or tomorrow we will go into such and such a town and spend a year

34. Matthews, *St. Philip Neri,* p. 41.

> there and trade and get gain"; whereas you do not know about tomorrow. What is your life? For you are a mist that appears for a little time and then vanishes. Instead you ought to say, "If the Lord wills, we shall live and we shall do this or that." As it is, you boast in your arrogance. All such boasting is evil. Whoever knows what is right to do and fails to do it, for him it is sin. (Jas 4:13–17)

That last line is a stinger. For this really was the state of the Church in the sixteenth-century Rome in which Philip lived—a failure to live out the Faith and do the right thing. Part of this may have been circumstantial—the Sack of 1527 at the hands of the troops of the Constable of Bourbon had left ruined palaces and profaned churches and a general lethargy of spirit. There was also the problem of ecclesial appointments being influenced by worldliness and nepotism. There were those who desired reform, but reform was still in the budding stage.[35]

Philip, for his part, was one of those breathing new breath into the religious atmosphere of the Church during this time of laxity. The brush fire of the Reformation was starting to spread from Germany, and we cannot help but think of Philip as one of the great Counter-Reformation saints in the Church.

35. Matthews, *St. Philip Neri,* p. 31.

The reality, however, is that Philip was, for the most part, insulated from this greater crisis by nature of his locality. Not that he didn't have his temptations to go off and do great things for Christ and his Church beyond the walls of Rome. In fact, the life of St. Francis Xavier harvesting souls in the foreign mission fields inspired Philip so much that he yearned to go to the Indies to labor for the kingdom. It was the counsel of a prophetic Cistercian, however, who informed Philip that "Rome will be your Indies," which solidified his vocation to a particular time and place. Philip considered this God's will and embraced his life and work at the local level.

Philip was also working in parallel with the likes of St. Ignatius of Loyola, who had founded the Society of Jesus (the Jesuits) in 1541. Philip admired Ignatius, and some of those whom Philip had converted even went off to join this new religious order. The two saints were markedly different in temperament and mission, and yet there was an affinity because they were laborers for the same Master. For as Newman notes:

> This was the office to which St. Philip wished to minister in India; but it was his zeal and charity that urged him, not his mature judgment; for the fierce conflicts, and the pastoral cares, and the rude publicity of such exalted duties, were

> unsuited to his nature; so he was kept at home for a different work.[36]

As mentioned earlier, Philip's *modus operandi* was that of informality—as both layman and priest—"doing good" in the here and now. His vocation was always a sort of nebulous one, as Philip himself was pliable to the bending of the Holy Spirit. Whereas the Jesuits were trained soldiers in God's army, Philip and his band of brothers were more akin to loose-knit mercenaries with less clearly defined marching orders.

Do not underestimate this temptation to draw you away from your vocation, however, for the devil uses all things—even seemingly good things—to tempt us from the path God has set out for us. There is an expression for us married folks: "If you ever wonder who you are meant to be married to, look at the name on the marriage certificate."

> Being asked by the Pharisees when the kingdom of God was coming, he answered them, "The kingdom of God is not coming with signs to be observed; nor will they say, 'Lo, here it is!' or 'There!' for behold, the kingdom of God is in the midst of you." (Lk 17:20–21)

36. Newman, "Sermon 12:2," no. 234.

Sometimes we think we must have everything preplanned and mapped out before we even start. Whether it is an apostolate, a parish initiative, or even just spreading the gospel as a layperson, the reality is that we need to take that first step out in faith to get the ball rolling. God honors that effort and will supply the grace. As a friend used to tell me, "Half the battle is won just by showing up." Perfection is the enemy of the good, and nothing ever goes completely according to plan anyway, so why not try something?

Philip didn't have an outline or a script when he struck up conversations on the streets of Rome with bankers and business owners—everything he did, he did from a place of prayer and with a "why not?" attitude. He also did not feel the need to wait for approval from ecclesiastical authorities to invite people into his room to read, pray, sing, and engage in conversations. It was an organic process that was completely natural and virtuous because Philip himself was natural and virtuous.

Sometimes we can get hung up on our qualifications to undertake such things and say, "I'm just a layman," or "I'm too young," or "I don't know my faith well enough." Or we can think, "when I'm less busy in my life, then I'll do such-and-such" and subsequently never start. Or maybe the place or circumstances in which we find ourselves are lacking in Catholic community, and we think to ourselves, "We should move to that place, then my faith will really deepen and we will have Catholic friends."

This is all a mirage. The Lord puts us in the time and place we are meant to be and expects us to work with what we have; what we lack, he will provide, as long as we have faith and trust in Providence. The Lord is looking for effort, not excuses.

The best place to start building up the kingdom is here, where you are. And the best time to start is now.

In Practice, Joyful Engagement

1. "Whoever knows what is right to do and fails to do it, for him it is sin." We are all guilty of having an inspiration that we don't follow up on, because we are either scared or we put it off for "tomorrow." What are practical ways in which you can become more engaged with doing what is right without hesitation?
2. Philip and St. Ignatius were "markedly different in temperament and mission, and yet there was an affinity because they were laborers for the same Master." Do you create division within your own Christian ranks, choosing differences in temperament or mission to divide rather than choosing to be united joyfully under the same Master? How can you foster a greater sense of joyful engagement that welcomes all laborers to share in the mission?
3. "God honors . . . effort and will supply the grace." Do you believe this? Does this belief help you move past your fears and plunge into Christian engagement with others? Do you regularly call on the Holy Spirit to supply you with the grace needed in each situation?

Chapter 8

Hidden Sanctity

A Love That Cannot Be Contained

The story of Philip's swollen heart is truly a peculiar event in the saint's life. When he was twenty-nine years old, Philip was praying in earnest for the gifts and graces of the Holy Spirit. It was said that he saw a "globe of fire which entered his mouth and sank down to his heart." This "fire of love" was physically hot and was manifested in Philip in painful ways.

After his death it was discovered that this divine indwelling had swollen his physical heart to almost twice its size and had broken two of his ribs. It also induced violent palpitations felt by those around him and allowed him to endure cold temperatures because of the heat this experience created within him.[37]

37. Matthews, *St. Philip Neri,* pp. 37–38.

Ecstasy was no stranger to Philip, and it seemed that for him it was not a matter of trying to stoke the fire of God's love within him in order to feel it, but to temper it lest it get out of control. For this fire burned so hot within him that he would tremble at the altar while celebrating Mass, his limbs would grow cold and numb while in prayer—a sign of ecstasy—and, as noted in many accounts of his life, the reading of frivolous books was necessary to "bring him back down to earth" lest he float away.

Most of us will have little moments in which we feel the love of God, are inspired to goodness or good works, or have little sparks of ignition light our hearts. We work to cultivate such love in prayer and adoration, and in charity. But these moments can be interspersed between more prolonged periods of forgetfulness, coldness, aridity, and lukewarmness. When we have obtained a modicum of virtue, there can also be the temptation to put our piety on display for others to see.

Love is the essence of the Christian life, and as St. Paul said, if a person does not have love, they are merely a resounding gong (see 1 Cor 13:1). Loving God and loving neighbor came naturally to Philip. Perhaps this is because he spent so much time in prayer; or maybe it was simply a supernatural grace. Philip's temperament was such that he was moved to tears often, though it was something he would try to conceal.

While he could keep his own sanctity close to his chest, his joy could not be hidden. Nor should it have been, for this joy "was wholly unconcealed, and diffused itself over all who came into contact with [him]."[38] It was not about him, because it did not come from him, but from God.

We live in an age hardly hidden—an age of tweets and shorts and posts, where our inner machinations are put on full display. When God affords us secrets and tender affections in the recesses of our hearts, we exploit for cheap likes and shares. Or, even more objectionable, we use such platforms to virtue-signal goodness—filming ourselves or others giving food to a hungry man on the street, or some other good deed used for show. In doing so we rob both the giver and receiver of their reward, which the Father bestows in secret for those who do them in secret (see Mt 6:3–4).

Newman writes this about Philip:

> When he became so famous in his old age, and every one was thinking of him mysteriously, and looking at him with awe, and solemnly repeating Father Philip's words and rehearsing Father Philip's deeds, and bringing strangers to see him, it was the most cruel of penances to him, and he was ever behaving himself ridiculously on purpose, and putting them out, from his intense hatred and impatience of being turned into a show. "He

38. Matthews, *St. Philip Neri,* p. 170.

> was always trying," says his biographer, "either by gestures, or motions, or words, or some facetious levity, to hide his great devotion; and when he had done any virtuous action, he would do something simple to cover it."[39]

There is a tension in that we are called as Christians to be a city on a hill, a lamp on a lampstand, but that we are not to let our right hand know what our left is doing in charity; to let our light shine before others that they may see our good works and thus glorify God while also being careful not to practice our righteousness in front of others to be seen by them (see Mt 5:14–16 and 6:1). The difference here is one of motivation, glorifying God and keeping yourself hidden is to be extolled; to glorify yourself at God's expense is to miss the mark and put yourself in a tenuous spiritual state.

There is nothing keeping us from asking for spiritual gifts such as those Philip received in extraordinary ways. Philip's motivations were pure, and the person asking for such gifts should also have purity of heart, for only the pure of heart shall see God (see Mt 5:8). We should not throw our pearls before swine, for the secret things belong to the Lord our God (see Dt 29:29). If the Lord gives us

39. Newman, "Sermon 12:2," no. 231.

gifts for the world to see, we are to use them for his glory, not ours.

Simple ejaculations hold great power: "Lord, I love you; help me to love you more"; "Speak, O Lord, for your servant is listening"; or "Here I am Lord, send me." That Philip received the burning globe of God's love was an extraordinary grace. But we too can receive this love when we rend our hearts and open ourselves up to the Lord in our secret room; whether or not it breaks our ribs physically is not important. For true love cannot be hidden; it cannot be contained.

In Practice, Joyful Love of God

1. "But when you give alms, do not let your left hand know what your right hand is doing, so that your alms may be in secret; and your Father who sees in secret will reward you." What is the value of a hidden good deed? Do you find a need to display your good deeds to others? If so, what is it that compels you to do so?
2. "He was always trying, either by gestures, or motions, or words, or some facetious levity, to hide his great devotion." Compare this description of Philip at the end of his life to St. Paul's words: "Love is patient and kind; love is not jealous or boastful; it is not arrogant or rude. Love does not insist on its own way; it is not irritable or resentful; it does not rejoice at wrong, but rejoices in the right. Love bears all things, believes all things, hopes all things, endures all things" (1 Cor 13:4–7).
3. "Philip's motivations were pure . . . only the pure of heart shall see God." Examine your motivations to love and serve God, to pray, to fast, to practice almsgiving. Can you say your motivations are pure? With honesty and humility, can you identify impure motivations in your heart that keep you from more complete joy in loving God?

Chapter 9

A Sign of Contradiction

He Who Seeks to Lose His Life Will Save It

Our Lord was not an easy man to put into a box. He picked grain on the Sabbath in contradiction to the Law. He was called a glutton and a drunkard. Even his own friends and disciples struggled to make sense of how he would usher in the restoration of Israel as King.

Our Lord Jesus might be taken by some as a radical reformer of the Jewish religion and way of life. No longer was it what someone eats that makes a person unclean, Jesus declared, but what comes out from a person's heart (see Mk 7:20–23). Those who declare corban (an offering to God among the ancient Hebrews) but neglect their father and mother in the process are not to be praised but brought to task (see Mk 7:11–13). There are many other such examples of a seemingly contradictory Jew bucking the system.

The Christian faith is replete with paradoxical teachings that seem to be contradictory: that Christ is both God and man (hypostatic union); that we are saved by both faith and works (see Jas 2:14–26); that he who seeks to lose his life will save it (see Mt 16:25). G. K. Chesterton said in *Orthodoxy*:

> If the great paradox of Christianity means anything it means this—that we must take the crown in our hands, and go hunting in dry places and dark corners of the earth until we find the one man who feels himself unfit to wear it. We have not got to crown the exceptional man who knows he can rule. Rather we must crown the much more exceptional man who knows he can't.[40]

Indeed, Jesus as Lord was doing "something new," as prophesized by the prophet Isaiah. And yet he insisted that until heaven and earth perish, not one jot or tittle will pass from the Law until all is accomplished (see Mt 5:18). The New Covenant was not an abrogation of the Old, but a bringing it to fulfillment.

In many ways we can see Philip following in the footsteps of our Lord doing a kind of "new thing" in Rome. If his goal was to bring in a draught of fish, what

40. G. K. Chesteron, *Orthodoxy* (Dover Publications, 2004), pp. 268–269.

difference did it make whether he used a line or a net to accomplish this task? But his doing so was not simply for novelty's sake, for he was merely being true to who he was, both in his temperament and particular calling.

But things that are out of the ordinary can sometimes spark suspicion. One of these was an act we take for granted today, but at the time was not commonplace, and that was the practice of receiving Communion frequently. Philip's confrere, a priest by the name of Buonsignore Cacciaguerra, who was known for his ardent faith, enthusiastically promoted the practice of daily Communion. Philip, who offered Mass every day, supported Cacciaguerra in this devotion. Not only that, but Philip, being true to his vocation as a priest, made himself available for confession at all times.

Clerics who were lax in their devotion and afraid such a custom would grow in popularity (and as a result, put more work on them) took Philip and Cacciaguerra's practice of frequent Communion as a threat. Two priests in particular, who had left their monasteries but retained their faculties and served as sacristans for the Archconfraternity of Charity headed up by a physician, Vincenzo Teccosi, leveled abuses and calumnies against Philip and his confrere. Their goal was to place seeds of doubt among Philip's followers. But the saint's patience was long-standing. He endured the humiliations and abuses from his persecutors, outlasting their ill-will and leading to their remorse and penitence in the process.

Under the reforms of Pope Paul IV, which sought to deal with such laxity and abuses within the Church, Philip found himself swept up as an innocent man with the guilty. He was called in to appear before the Pope's vicar in 1557 under the charge of being an "introducer of novelties and an ambitious man, and of forming a sect." As a result of these charges, he was forbidden to continue the exercise of the Oratory until new permission could be given, he could not go about Rome in the company of others, and he was suspended from hearing confessions for a fortnight.[41]

Philip submitted in obedience, though it must have been torturous for him. He enlisted everyone he knew to pray about the situation, and one day a religious appeared at the Oratory who prophesized that the persecution would soon end and those that opposed Philip's work would be punished. A few months later the Pope's vicar died suddenly, and as a result Paul IV had a change of heart and reconsidered Philip's innocence. The pope rescinded all the aforementioned prohibitions, and the work of the Oratory resumed.[42]

41. Matthews, *St. Philip Neri,* p. 98.
42. Matthews, *St. Philip Neri,* pp. 98–100.

In order to become a saint, such docility and deference to humiliation, and even persecution, must be cultivated. We should not be afraid to follow the will of God for our lives, discerned in prayer and through trusted guidance, even when we know it will meet resistance. For we are in company with the Christ, of whom it was said in Scripture by Simeon: "Behold, this child is set for the fall and rising of many in Israel, and for a sign that is spoken against" (Lk 2:34).

In Practice, Joyful Docility to God's Will

1. "But things that are out of the ordinary can sometimes spark suspicion." At times we may be called by the Lord to act in contradiction to societal norms. A joyful docility to his will does not always come naturally. What are ways in which you can you plant yourself firmly in trust, joy, and docility?

2. "He endured the humiliations and abuses from his persecutors, outlasting their ill-will and leading to their remorse and penitence in the process." Our joyful docility reaps the highest rewards. Do you believe this? When humiliated or persecuted, can you see past the pain and trust in the Lord's will? Do you trust that the Lord can use your joyful docility in tough times as a valuable lesson to others?

3. "He enlisted everyone he knew to pray about the situation." Philip relied on the community of believers around him to support him in his trials. Do you attempt to go through your trials alone? Do you see the value in sharing your sorrows with trusted family, friends, or confidants? Do you believe in the true power of prayer?

S·Philippus·Nerius·Conf·et·Oratorii·Congreg·Instit·

Chapter 10

The School of Christian Mirth

Like a Beacon on a Hill

When you have tasted even a sweet droplet from the dew permeating heaven, nothing on earth can compare. This can make life difficult, for it puts things in their true light. St. Thomas Aquinas, when he had experienced a heavenly revelation three months before his death, noted to his friend and secretary: "The end of my labors has come. All that I have written appears to be as so much straw after the things that have been revealed to me." It was not because he regretted writing the *Summa Theologiae*, for Christ revealed to him in another mystical experience the highest honor: "You have written well of me, Thomas."[43]

43. Peggy Frye, "When St. Thomas Aquinas Likened His Work to Straw, Was That a Retraction of What He Wrote?" Catholic Answers, accessed March 25, 2025, www.catholic.com/qa/when-st-thomas-aquinas-likened-his-work-to-straw-was-that-a-retraction-of-what-he-wrote.

In a similar vein to that of St. Thomas, Philip's humility led him to burn all his writing before his death. No written compilation of his methodology of prayer or philosophy of life remains, though after he died his followers did compile various short maxims attributed to him. Perhaps it is because words cannot do justice to the majesty of God's kingdom, and all pales in comparison to the reality of his court.

As Christian disciples we attempt to carry out during our tenure, however imperfectly, what we pray in the Lord's prayer, "Thy will be done, on earth as it is in heaven" (Mt 6:10). As disciples, we seek to leave a legacy here on earth, not for our own glory, but for the kingdom. In doing so, we desire that our prayers are actualized and the work continues after we are gone until he comes again in glory.

The Oratory was Philip's living monument, his legacy, and the testament to his work as a disciple of Jesus Christ. The Oratory was not a school in the strict sense, nor a hospital, nor a vocation house, nor charitable organization. Its first incarnation came about at the behest of Philip's confessor, Persiano Rosa, as a loose federation of a dozen laymen who would gather together in a hired house for common prayer and spiritual conversations. The structure, the place in which they gathered, was incidental to the mission of the confraternity, which maintained its simple ideals of providing an *opportunity* to gather for prayer, Mass, readings, and conversation. Again, as the saying goes, "Food is the icing, and company is the cake."

The earliest incarnation of the Oratory also adopted an informal mission beyond personal edification and leisure—that of charity, specifically to serve and house convalescents. This charity, and the beginnings of such spiritual practices as the Forty Hours devotion, formed the backbone of this loose-knit fraternity of those attracted to the practice of "doing good." It is noteworthy that Philip was in fact still a layman during this period. He would fortify those who gathered at the Oratory with little sermons he delivered while still in this state. It was only at the urging of his confessor that he pursued holy orders, being ordained to the priesthood in 1551.

Becoming a priest afforded Philip one of his greatest means of conversion of sinners— that of a confessor. He heard confession for hours each day in the church, but as his reputation grew, he also heard them in his room—sometimes up to forty confessions before even making it down to the church.[44] The practice of "meeting in a room," combined with afternoon conversations and evening prayer, was the essence of what would later be known as the Oratory.

44. Matthews, *St. Philip Neri,* pp. 55–56.

In the age we live in today, when scandal and abuse in the priestly ranks is so often in the news, Philip's practice of meeting with young men in his private room (and even leaving a key for them) may seem inappropriate or lacking discretion. However, it should instead be a testament to the saint's character that this was no cause for scandal. For like David the psalmist, the Lord had given Philip a pure heart (see Ps 51:10). It is a temptation of our perverted generation to cast any shadow on the saint's good sense, for Philip's purity was beyond reproach and afforded him such informal opportunities. Abusing such trust would not have even crossed his mind, earning him the noble affections of such young men whom he brought into the Lord's fold.

The spoken word was integral to the composition of the Oratory, yet the simplicity and practicality with which discourses were delivered was a noted departure from the reputation of homiletics in Philip's day. "What can I hear in sermons!" laments Cardinal Pietro Bembo, "but Doctor Subtilis striving with Doctor Angelicus, and Aristotle coming in as a third to decide the quarrel." The "familiar four" topics covered by sermons at the Oratory were:

> first an exposition on some point of the spiritual reading which preceded them, and therefore impromptu; the next would be on some text of

> Holy Scripture; the third on ecclesiastical history, and the fourth on the lives of the saints. Each sermon lasted half an hour, when a bell was rung and the preacher at once ceased speaking.[45]

We sometimes think that in order to "do something" we need to found an apostolate or a nonprofit, replete with a board of directors, officers, and cash. The fact is, however, that the school of Christian mirth begins in our own homes. It is formed during morning and evening prayer with our spouses and children. It is community which is cultivated at the kitchen table during supper. It is the home base from which they learn charity and love of neighbor. It is the learning and playing together which strengthens the bonds of the Christian family.

This school of love remains fixed and rooted in a particular community, but that does not mean that the Christian should be content to always harbor safely within its walls. For Philip, the "going out" was integral to the "bringing in," even though this all took place in a constricted geographic locale (Rome). The ripple effect from this localized apostolate reached all corners of the globe after his death.

45. Henry Sebastian Bowden, "The Oratory of St. Philip Neri," in *The Catholic Encyclopedia,* vol. 11 (Robert Appleton Company, 1911). https://www.newadvent.org/cathen/11272a.htm.

We simply cannot underestimate the potential our love and charity (which begins in the home) will have on the world, for "no eye has seen, nor ear heard, nor the heart of man conceived, what God has prepared for those who love him" (1 Cor 2:9). It does not have to be complicated or formal, but it can be creative: inviting a coworker over for dinner and introducing them to the Faith; reaching out to a divorced or widowed parishioner for tea; welcoming a priest into your home and inviting them to celebrate Mass. Even something like a Ping-Pong tournament or a backyard barbeque can be an opportunity to evangelize. When joy and mirth is the mark of a Christian home, it becomes like a beacon on a hill, a school of virtue, and a harbor of charity.

In Practice, Spreading Joy

1. "The school of Christian mirth begins in our own homes." Philip began a "home" in which community could gather. The building didn't matter, the gathering did. Do you foster community within your own family, in your own home? What are practical ways in which you can foster a better community of prayer, learning, playing, and eating together?
2. "For Philip, the 'going out' was integral to the 'bringing in,' even though this all took place in a constricted geographic locale." The beauty of community you foster in your home must overflow into the world. Consider how your family can be beacons of light and truth in a smog-covered world.
3. Our Christian love and charity "does not have to be complicated or formal, but it can be creative." What does Christian creativity mean to you? How can you creatively spread joy in your family, parish, and community?

Chapter 11

A New Evangelization

Called to Recover

A major focus since the Second Vatican Council has been evangelization—or rather, a kind of *re-evangelization*. Just as the Lord sought out the lost sheep of Israel as his primary mission, the Church has realized that those who have been baptized and sacramentalized in the Church have nonetheless fallen prey to a de-Christianized culture. Their catechism is in many cases rudimentary and feeble against the tsunami-like forces of an unbelieving and religiously apathetic age. They may be "low-hanging fruit" in the vineyard, but that does not mean the work is easy.

Pope St. Paul VI observed that evangelization is a duty of all Christians, but that in order to carry out this task we need to know Jesus Christ in a different way from what we were taught as children and carry out this task with greater force and urgency. Pope St. John Paul II notes that:

> Whole countries and nations where religion and the Christian life were formerly flourishing and capable of fostering a viable and working community of faith, are now put to a hard test, and in some cases, are even undergoing a radical transformation, as a result of a constant spreading of religious indifference, secularism and atheism .
>
> . . . Only a re-evangelization can assure the growth of a clear and deep faith.[46]

And Pope Benedict XVI said that a "hermeneutic of discontinuity and rupture" must be counteracted by a 'hermeneutic of reform,' of renewal in the continuity of the one subject-Church which the Lord has given to us."[47]

What are these three postconciliar popes positing? That it is our *job*, as laypeople, to do the work of saints? Well, *yes*. This is the *universal call to holiness*, another major theme of Vatican II: that such holiness is not reserved for priests and religious alone, but that by virtue of a layperson's baptism, they too are called to labor in the vineyard to propagate the Gospel.

46. Benedict XVI, Apostolic Letter *Ubicumque et Semper* (September 21, 2010), www.vatican.va.

47. Synod of Bishops, *The New Evangelization for the Transmission of the Christian Faith*, General Secretariat of the Synod of Bishops, 2012, www.vatican.va.

Though he lived almost half a millennium before the council, no one exemplifies this evangelical spirit more than St. Philip Neri. For he did not regard his state in life as a layman (prior to his ordination) as an impediment that would keep him from exercising his baptismal duty. As he was wont to say: "Well brothers, when shall we begin to do good?"[48]

The mission of Christianizing pagan lands in imitation of St. Francis Xavier or St. Ignatius of Loyola was not what God was calling Philip to. Their vocation was to bring the light of faith to a dark world; for Philip, his calling was to simply reignite the lamp that had begun to smolder due to negligence and apathy. Because of this, his sacramental weapon, as Newman calls it, was of a different sort:

> He was kept at home, in the very heart of Christendom, not to evangelize, but to recover; and his instrument of conversion was, not Baptism, but Penance. The Confessional was the seat and seal of his peculiar Apostolate. Hence, as St. Francis Xavier baptized his tens of thousands, Philip was, every day and almost every hour, for forty-five years, restoring, teaching, encouraging, and guiding penitents along the narrow way of salvation.[49]

48. Matthews, *St. Philip Neri,* p. 41.
49. Newman, "Sermon 12:2," nos. 234–235.

Of course, the hearing of confessions necessitated that Philip receive holy orders, a vocation he was resistant to until his own confessor urged him toward it. In this way Philip's humility and docility to the Holy Spirit equipped him to wield a mighty axe through his evangelical ministry. Most of those in need of repentance and metanoia in his domestic mission field were baptized Christians who were only one good confession away from the kingdom of heaven.

Of course, hearty teaching and compelling catechesis helped to fill the empty stomachs of these now-reformed men and women. But their appetite was first whetted through contrition. For it is in contrition that a person realizes how hungry they truly are, and only then do they seek to be filled. In making confession—and by extension, himself—so readily available to others, Philip set a place for them at the table of reconciliation and confirmed the engagement with the Lord of Hosts. There they encounter Christ in Philip's person, who so gently brings them back into the fold and enlivens in them a desire to don once again the pure white robes of their baptism and begin anew.

Our age is not so unprecedented (for, as they say, history repeats itself), but it does offer unique challenges to the modern disciple. For every convert coming into the Catholic Faith, six are leaving. One in five people who were raised Catholic now say they have no religious affiliation, while ten percent identify with evangelical denominations and five percent with mainline denominations.[50] These are baptized believers, welcomed into the family of God, who have not made their faith their own. They may have received all their sacraments, been taught the faith, or attended Catholic school. But at the end of the day, they have been handed the pearl of great price and have put it on a shelf.

In some ways, this spiritual apathy is not unlike sixteenth-century Rome. As Cardinal Newman notes:

> The Germans and Spaniards had besieged, taken, and sacked it, with excesses and outrages so horrible, that it is thought to have suffered less from the Goths and Huns than from troops nominally Christian. Its external splendour has never been recovered down to this day; its churches were spoiled and defaced; its convents plundered; its Cardinals, Bishops, monks, and nuns, treated with the most extreme indignities, and many of them murdered; and sacrileges committed innumerable.[51]

Perhaps the Christian Roman citizenry was leveled a blow so staggering it simply stayed on the mat; whether it was a kind of cultural PTSD or the fulfillment of a divine

50. Pew Research Center, *America's Changing Religious Landscape*, May 12, 2015, chap. 2, "Religious Switching and Intermarriage," https://www.pewresearch.org/religion/2015/05/12/chapter-2-religious-switching-and-intermarriage/.

51. Newman, "Sermon 12:2," no. 232.

judgment is for historians to judge. Their love and zeal had grown cold, and some were even enticed by the novelty of the newly minted Lutheran sect. Suffice it to say that the environment in which Philip took up his calling was one of lackluster despondency, desperate for renewal.

Philip was called "not to evangelize, but to *recover*."[52] And so are we. This is the "new" evangelization. Relativism, materialism, and religious antipathy are the rust steadily eroding the iron pillars upholding the Judeo-Christian West. Yet, for baptized Christians, they are given everything they need to carry out their duty to recover what has been lost and restore what has been so slovenly neglected. They do not need to board a plane or a ship destined to far away pagan lands (though some may indeed be called by God to do so); they need only step outside their front door and encounter their neighbor or a stranger on the street to realize the field of mission is fertile. They need not be a theologian or a trained apologist or even a priest. Through basic catechesis, bold witness, and docility to the Holy Spirit, they too can lay claim to the bounty of souls ahead, as Philip did by calling others to repentance.

The person who has been handed the Faith as a child and who has left it in a corner is in many ways harder to

52. Newman, "Sermon 12:2," nos. 234–35.

convert than the most hostile pagan. For they hate (or shrug their shoulders at) what they think they know, as Archbishop Fulton Sheen famously said—that is, they hate what they perceive the Catholic Church to be.[53] They retain their muscle memory of a childhood faith that in many ways has become irrelevant to their everyday life in the modern world. Few demands have been placed on them by the Church, and even fewer reasons given to recognize their wretched state as a sinner worthy of damnation. Like any good consumer, they have been presented the Catholic Faith devoid of fervent belief as a kind of cringe-worthy country club and have rightfully exercised their "freedom of choice" to take a hard pass.

Cardinal Emmanuel Célestin Suhard, archbishop of Paris from 1940 to 1949, said, "To be a witness does not consist in engaging in propaganda, nor even in stirring people up, but in being a living mystery. It means to live in such a way that *one's life would not make sense if God did not exist.*"[54] For while Francis Xavier was baptizing throngs of souls hungry for the bread of life, the Christian engaged in the work of the new evangelization today is

53. "There are not a hundred people in America who hate the Catholic Church. There are millions of people who hate what they wrongly believe to be the Catholic Church—which is, of course, quite a different thing." Fulton Sheen, foreword to *Radio Replies*, vol. 1 (Radio Replies Press,1938) p. 6.

54. Michael Garvey, "Believing: Lives That Make Sense," *Notre Dame Magazine*, August 5, 2010, https://magazine.nd.edu/stories/believing-lives-that-make-sense/.

repossessing souls from Satan in the single digits. He is pulling bodies onto the ark, one by one and in dribs and drabs. For every person being saved, six more go forth to their perdition.

And yet, for those souls being ransomed, their personal freedom song from the bondage of slavery and death echoes that of the Israelites through their adoption and deliverance by Yahweh. At the hands of a witness, they were at first moved by curiosity ("Why does this man live the way he does?"), then by proximate exposure ("Why does he love like this? Where does his joy come from?"), onward to contrition when shown his true self ("God, be merciful to me a sinner"), and finally restoration and reconciliation in the confessional ("Go and sin no more"). As Catholic Christians, they have been born again (see Jn 1:3).

Who is that witness who bears light to the truth? That person is you. Whether a single man or woman, a married man or woman, a priest or a religious, the call to holiness is *universal*. You are not exempt. You do not have to wait for permission. You have all the grace you need to do the work of a witness, for Christ's saints have followed him and gone before you to show you a way. As St. Paul says, "In my flesh I complete what is lacking in Christ's afflictions for the sake of his body, that is, the church" (Col 1:24).

Where we have holes, grace fills in to do the heavy lifting. Perfection is not necessary. Waiting for the right time to start the work of reclamation is not necessary. For if you were to have the faith of a mustard seed, you would move mountains; nothing would be impossible for you (see Mt 17:20). He who begins, as the adage goes, does half the work. And then, like Philip, you will be the one turning to your fellow laborers and asking, "Well then, brothers, when shall we begin to do good?"

In Practice, Joyful Evangelism

1. "Philip was, every day and almost every hour, for forty-five years, restoring, teaching, encouraging, and guiding penitents along the narrow way of salvation." Effective evangelism takes patience, constancy, and belief that small steps lead to great rewards. Do you believe in your mission in this world, no matter how small and insignificant it may seem?
2. "It is in contrition that a person realizes how hungry they truly are, and only then do they seek to be filled." Are you a joyful recipient of the sacrament of confession? Do you quietly witness to your family a joyful commitment to contrition and penance?
3. We have a "duty to recover what has been lost and restore what has been so slovenly neglected." To recover the Faith means to rediscover its beauty, to relearn its teachings, to review it through a new lens that illuminates its truths in an astonishing way. Do you commit to rediscovering your faith through prayer and study so you can be an effective and joyful evangelizer?

Afterword

St. Philip Neri died on May 26, 1595, at the age of seventy-nine. While Philip was alive, Clement VIII said that Philip would one day be canonized, and indeed he was beatified on May 25, 1615, by Pope Paul V. You would be hard-pressed to find a person in Rome during that time who was not convinced of his sanctity, such was his reputation.

But Philip, for his part, knew better. His admission to his friend Cardinal Charles Borromeo, just two weeks before his death, was that "I never was worthy, for I have never done any good."[55] This was a man who was said to have never committed a mortal sin, who had wrought great works of charity and inspired countless conversions. A man who heard confessions for hours on end without even the slightest complaint, and whose heart literally swelled to twice its original size, breaking ribs in the process, because he was so in love with God.

I never was worthy, for I have never done any good. And he believed it with all his heart.

55. Matthews, *St. Philip Neri,* p. 224.

This is the paradox of humility, a sign of contradiction: for we see ourselves as we really are in contrast with the overwhelming goodness of God. For the Holy Spirit, like a dove, can only rest on the peaceable and humble. The slightest movement of pride or self-love is enough to send him to flight.

Chesterton wrote of this paradox of the Christian faith, which was exemplified in the life of Philip, this "Apostle of Joy":

> It was not enough that slaves who stole wine inspired partly anger and partly kindness. We must be much more angry with theft than before, and yet much kinder to thieves than before. There was room for wrath and love to run wild. And the more I considered Christianity, the more I found that while it had established a rule and order, the chief aim of that order was to give room for good things to run wild.[56]

When I reflect on the life of St. Philip Neri, I see a man who "gave room for good things to run wild." He was a man of deep prayer in love with the Lord, both of which he took deadly seriously. And yet he did not take himself seriously at all, whether in shaving off half his beard to look the fool or bearing with the indignity of others for his attachment to joke books. He was always

56. Chesteron, *Orthodoxy*, pp. 213–214.

putting others before himself, living and suffering for them. He was psychologically deft, a man of men, both gentle and fierce as occasion dictated. Like a fire fully consumed which leaves nothing but the finest coating of white ash in the furnace, Philip (and any of his writings) at his death became like a funeral pyre—disappearing and leaving no trace of himself at all, but only Christ.

And yet, his legacy lives on. Congregations of the Oratory, still bearing the fruits of Philip's "lay informality," may be found throughout Italy, Spain, Germany, Austria, Switzerland, Poland, England, and North and South America today. Oratorians are bound by no formal vow save for that of the bond of charity. They bear the imprint of their founder in their joy and apostolic zeal.

Philip is to me both a spiritual confrere and a quixotic taskmaster: to be under his tutelage is to have your pretensions crucified before you, your table of assumptions flipped upside down, and your sins laid bare. But it is also to learn the nature of love bound by the rule of charity, where wrath and love are given free rein to run wild. You do not sit at the feet of Philip Neri to learn to become like him. For in becoming his disciple, he raises you up so that you become more like yourself.

We live in a culture in which there is a dearth of joy. We are replete in counterfeits, of course—the emptiness of superficial connections and encounters, the contraceptive nature of virtual media, the consumeristic promises proven time and time again to be empty shells and mirages. Our humor is crass and our entertainment banal, because this is what the world knows and is all it has to offer. And we accept it for lack of anything better. What people seek in their heart of hearts is a well that does not run dry, living water—in short, we seek the Christ, the embodiment of God. The authentic man.

The kingdom of God is within you, as we are reminded in Luke's Gospel. We have everything we need to discover that kingdom within ourselves and be saved—the true Faith, the sacraments, the Mass, and each other. But sometimes we need that person that God raises up in a certain time and in a particular place to inspire us to sell what we have and buy the pearl—that friend, that coach . . . that saint.

Joy is not an end in itself but a byproduct of the Christian life fully lived. It is an indication or litmus that you are on the right path, for the person with joy—even in the midst of suffering—has found the pearl of great price and knows its worth. When you know Christ, you know joy.

Philip would be the first to say that he is but one person among many throughout history pointing the way to the Father through Christ. He may do it with jokes, with laughter and merriment, with singing, and with joy.

He may be unconventional, or even uncouth. But the goal is the same: to get you to heaven, and to bring your friends. Your Rome is here. Your century is this one.

When shall we begin to do good? I'd say now is as good a time as any.

Art Attribution

Chapter 1

Giacomo Pavia. *Portrait of Saint Philip Neri at 15 Years Old*. Intaglio engraving. 18th Century. Civi Museum of Lodi. Public Domain. https://commons.wikimedia.org.

Chapter 2

Brianne Schulze. *St. Philip Neri*. Oil on Canvas. www.brieschulze.com.

Chapter 3

Unknown artist. *Saint Philip Neri*. Intaglio print. Wellcome Collection, reference no. 6845i. Public Domain. https://wellcomecollection.org.

Chapter 4

Giovanni Marco Pitteri after Giovanni Battista Piazzetta. *Saint Philip Neri*. Line engraving, 1700-1799. Wellcome Collection, reference no. 6844i. Public Domain. https://wellcomecollection.org.

Chapter 5

Marcantonio Franceschini. *Angel Heals St. Philip Neri*. Church of San Filippo Neri, Genoa. www.alamy.com.

Chapter 6
Unknown artist. *Saint Philip Neri.* Church of San Filippo Neri, Catania. 1937. www.dreamstime.com.

Chapter 7
Carlo Dolci. *Saint Philip Neri.* 1645 or 1646. www.alamy.com.

Chapter 8
Hermann Hutterer. *St. Filippo Neri in Ecstasy* (after Guido Reni, 1614). Oil on canvas. Copy of the original. Located at St. Roch Church, Vienna. Public Domain. www.dreamstime.com.

Chapter 9
A.G. Faldoni, after Tommaso Conca. *Saint Philip Neri.* Engraving. Wellcome Collection, reference no. 6854i. Public Domain. https://wellcomecollection.org.

Chapter 10
Unknown artist. *Philip Neri.* www.alamy.com (Image ID: AA0PXC).

Chapter 11
Sebastiano Conca. *The Madonna Appearing to Saint Philip Neri.* Oil on canvas, 1740. Indianapolis Museum of Art, Newfields Collection. Public Domain. https://collections.discovernewfields.org.